ⓑelgrade theatre
coventry

C000151107

Head/Case

by Ron Hutchinson

A Belgrade Theatre Production first presented in October 2004 at
The Swan Theatre, Stratford.

Coventry City Council

ARTS COUNCIL
ENGLAND

THIS PROJECT IS BEING
PART-FUNDED BY THE
EUROPEAN COMMUNITY

belgrade theatre
coventry

Head/Case

The Company

Cast

Tracy	**Claire Cogan**
Julia	**Sarah Cattle**
Jimmy	**Jonjo O'Neill**

Creative Team

Writer	**Ron Hutchinson**
Director	**Caroline Hunt**
Designer	**Tom Piper**
Composer	**John O'Hara**
Lighting Designer	**Ben Ormerod**
Movement	**Kevin Walton**
Producer	**Jane Hytch**
Assistant Director	**Lucy Taylor**

Original Production Team

Production Manager	**Barry Hope**
Company Stage Manager	**Lianne Bruce**
Deputy Stage Manager on the book	**Sara Austin-Wells**
Assistant Stage Manager	**Elizah Jackson**

Theatre Management

Chairman	**David Burbidge OBE DL**
Artistic Director & Chief Executive	**Hamish Glen**
Executive Director	**Joanna Reid**

Thank You

Nick Bouton, Miriam Cooper and Keiran Lagan for their valuable work during the development of Head/Case, Dr Robert Meech, and all at Headway House Bristol for their help and generosity.

First performance presented by the Belgrade Theatre, Coventry on 14 October 2004 at the Swan Theatre, Stratford-upon-Avon.

Cast

Claire Cogan Tracy

Claire was born in Northern Ireland and moved to England in 1990. After graduating from Royal Holloway University with a degree in Drama and Theatre Studies in 1997, she moved back to Ireland and lived in Belfast for the next six years.

While in Ireland her stage credits included *Factory Girls* (Lyric Theatre, Belfast), *LAGS* (Battersea Arts Centre), *A Midsummer Night's Dream* (Old Museum Arts Centre, Belfast), *Shapeshifters* (Peacock Theatre, Dublin) and three Theatre In Education tours for TEAM, REPLAY and KINETIC. Film and TV credits include *Wild About Harry* (Scala Productions), *The McKeever Show* (Wild Rover Productions) and *Everything You Know Is Wrong* for Green Inc Productions.

Sarah Cattle Julia

Theatre credits include: *Skellig* (Young Vic), *Holes in the Skin* (Chichester Festival), *Black Milk* (Royal Court), *Terrorism* (Royal Court), *Inside Out* (Clean Break), *Neutralized* (Royal Court), *Made of Stone* (Young Writers Festival), *Boeing, Boeing* (Lyceum, Crewe), *Peril at End House* (Grand, Wolverhampton), *American Days* (Mill Studio) and *A Midsummer Night's Dream* (Chilworth Manor).

Film includes: *Silent Cry* (Peter La Terriere) and *My Life as a Fairytale* (Hallmark).

Television includes: *The Royal* (Yorkshire TV), *Bodies* (Hat Trick Productions), *Rockface* (BBC Scotland) and *Linda Green* (Red Productions).

Jonjo O'Neill Jimmy

Theatre credits include: *Paradise Lost* (Northampton Theatre), *A View From the Bridge* (Birmingham Rep), *Murmuring Judges* (Birmingham Rep), *Observe the Sons of Ulster Marching Towards the Somme* (Pleasance), *Dolly West's Kitchen* (Leicester Haymarket), *Half a Sixpence* (West Yorkshire Playhouse), *Translations* (Palace Theatre Watford/tour), *Dick Whittington* (Sadler's Wells), *Of Thee I Sing* (Bridewell Theatre), *The Frogs* (Nottingham Playhouse/tour) and *Refuge* (Royal Court).

Film and television credits include: *I Fought the Law* (BBC, N Ireland), *Fakers* (Kleparski & Bee Prods), *Murphy's Law: Manic Munday* (Tiger Aspect), *Bay College* (BBC Wales), *A Touch of Frost* (YTV), *Charlie's Angels* (Alomo), *Band of Brothers* (Dreamworks), *Risk* (Risk Productions), *Thin Ice* (BBC), *Hol by City* (BBC), *Sunburn* (BBC), *Extremely Dangerous* (Patagonia Films), *Flux: Out for Nowt* (HatTrick).

Production

Ron Hutchinson Writer

Latest theatre work includes *Rat in the Skull* (revival, Duke of York's Theatre 1995); an adaptation of Mikhail Bulgakov's *Flight* at the National Theatre 1997; *Burning Issues*, Hampstead Theatre Club 1999; *Beau!*, Theatre Royal, Bath, national tour and Haymarket, Leicester Square 2001; *LAGS*, national tours 2002- 03; *Believers*, for Playbox Young People's Theatre, 2003; *Moonlight and Magnolias*, Goodman Theatre, Chicago 2004, to be produced off-Broadway by the Manhattan Theatre Club, Spring 2005.

Mr Hutchinson lives in Los Angeles, where he is a writer/producer for features and television. Winner of an Emmy for Ben Kingsley's *Murderers Among Us; The Simon Wiesenthal Story*, 1989, his latest projects include *Traffic*, nominated for three Emmys in 2004 and rewrites on Fox Pictures' remake of *Flight of the Phoenix*, to be released 2005.

Caroline Hunt Director

Caroline trained at LAMDA.

Caroline was founder and artistic director of CV ONE Theatre Company, a new writing company at the Coventry Belgrade Studio where new work included *Into Europe* and *Anchorman* by Ron Hutchinson, and *A Little Like Drowning* by Anthony Minghella. Other productions include: *A Man and Some Women*, *How She Loves Him*, *A Show of Strength*, *Blavatsky's Tower*, Moira Buffini, *My Mother Said I Never Should* by Charlotte Keatley, *The Beau* by Ron Hutchinson (Theatre Royal Bath and Theatre Royal Haymarket London), *A Taste of Honey* by Shelagh Delaney (National Theatre), *Mary Stuart* by Dacia Maraini and *League of Youth* (Bristol Old Vic) plus *Lags* by Ron Hutchinson.

John O'Hara Composer

John is a graduate of the Royal Northern College of Music. His work spans a wide range of styles including performances with the Halle, the Royal Liverpool Philharmonic Orchestra, Rambert Dance Company, Kalengo Percussion Ensemble and the Lindsay Kemp Dance Company. He was the resident composer / musical director at the Bristol Old Vic for eleven years and in that time worked on most in-house productions, titles include: *Macbeth*, *King Lear*, *Hamlet*, *Moll Flanders*, *The Chimes*, *A Christmas Carol*, *The Beggar's Opera*, *Up the Feeder Down the Mouth*, *Blues Brother Soul Sisters*, *Maid Marian the Musical*, *The Rise and Fall of Little Voice*, *Stone Free*, *Too Much Too Young*. Other theatre work includes: the National Theatre, Lyric Theatre Hammersmith, Leicester Haymarket, Liverpool Playhouse and the Royal Exchange.

Television commissions include: *A Miracle on the River Kwai*, *History in Action*, *Nick's Quest*, *Run With the Ball* and *Time and Tide*. John has just completed a children's opera for the Welsh National Opera and is currently scoring, conducting and performing with Ian Anderson (Jethro Tull) on his Rubbing Elbows and Orchestral projects.

Tom Piper Designer

Tom graduated from Trinity College, Cambridge before training at the Slade School of Art in theatre design.

Theatre designs for the Royal Shakespeare Company include: *The Tempest*, *Henry VI Parts 1, 2 & 3*, *Richard III*, *Romeo and Juliet*, *A Midsummer Night's Dream*, *A Month in the Country*, *Troilus and Cressida*, *Measure for Measure*, *Bartholomew Fair*, *The Broken Heart*, *Spring Awakening*, *A Patriot for Me*, *Much Ado About Nothing*, *The Spanish Tragedy*, *Hamlet* and *King Lear*. Designs for the National Theatre include: *The Birthday Party*, *Blinded by the Sun*, and *Oh! What a Lovely War* (RNT Mobile tour and Camden Roundhouse). Other work includes: *Babette's Feast* (Royal Opera House); *Protection*, *Meeting Myself Coming Back* (Soho Theatre); *Just Between Ourselves* (Theatre Royal Bath); *Pants* (Dundee Rep); *Frame 312* (Donmar); *Mother Courage* (Olympia Theatre, Dublin); *A Lie of the Mind* (Donmar); *Denial* (Bristol Old Vic); *Miss Julie* (Haymarket Theatre); *Helpless* (Donmar Warehouse); *Hedda Gabler* (Plymouth Theatre Royal and No 1 tour); *Penny for A Song* (Whitehall and UK tour); *The Spirit of Annie Ross* (the Gate Theatre, Dublin); *Disposing of the Body* (Hampstead Theatre); *The Frogs* (Nottingham Playhouse); *Stiff!* (Lyceum, Edinburgh and tour); The American Imports Season including *Three Days of Rain* (Donmar Warehouse); *Mince* (Dundee Rep), *Dealer's Choice* (Theater In Der Josefstadt, Vienna); *Scissor Happy* (Duchess Theatre); *Wallace and Gromit – A Grand Night Out* (Peacock Theatre and national tour); *Kindertransport* (Vaudeville, Watford and Soho Theatre Company); *Four Plays Four Weeks* (Re-opening Season at Soho Theatre); *The Crucible* and *Six Characters in Search of an Author* (both Abbey Theatre, Dublin); *Backpay* (Storming Festival, Royal Court); *Cockroach, Who?* (Royal Court); *Waking*, *Tulipfutures*, *Ripped*, *My Goat* and *Rockstation* (all Soho Theatre Company); *The Master Builder* (Lyceum, Edinburgh); *Endgame*, *Dumbstruck*, *Macbeth*, *Cinderella* and *Jack and the Beanstalk* (all Tron Theatre, Glasgow); *The Price* (York Theatre Royal); *The Way of the World* (Lyric Hammersmith); *The Duchess of Malfi* (Wyndham's, Greenwich and tour); *Sweet Panic* and *The Philanderer* (both Hampstead Theatre); *The Cherry Orchard* (Nottingham Playhouse); *The Dark River*, *Cat With Green Violin*, *His Majesty*, *We the Undersigned* and *Mrs Warren's Profession* (all Orange Tree Theatre, Richmond); *Les Liaisons Dangereuses* (Bristol Old Vic), *The Duchess of Malfi*, *Jack and the Beanstalk* and *Twelfth Night* (all Dundee Rep) and *Sweet Panic* (Duke of York's).

Tom has won the London Fringe Best Design Award twice. He was Chloe Obolensky's assistant for Peter Brook's production of *The Tempest* and the Design Consultant for the new Soho Theatre in Dean Street. He is an Associate Artist of the Royal Shakespeare Company.

Ben Ormerod Lighting Designer

RSC: *Julius Caesar, Henry V,The Two Gentlemen of Verona, The Revenger's Tragedy*. This season: *The Dog in a Manger, Tamar's Revenge, House of Desire* and *Pedro de Urdemalas*. Other theatre includes: *Rose Rage* (Brooklyn Academy/Chicago/West End/tour/Watermill), *A Midsummer Night's Dream* (Brooklyn/West End/tour/Watermill), *Macbeth* (West End), *The Constant Wife* (West End/tour), *The Marquise, The Circle* (no 1 tours), *Remembrance of Things Past, Uncle Vanya, Bent, Accidental Death of an Anarchist* and *The Winter's Tale* (National Theatre), *John Gabriel Borkmann* (ETT), *The Father* (Athens), *The Beauty Queen of Leenane* (Broadway/Sydney/Toronto/West End/Druid Theatre). Ballet: *See Blue Through* (Phoenix Dance Company and Ballet Gulbenkian), *Tender Hooks* (Ballet Gulbenkian); *I Remember Red* (Cullberg Ballet); *A Streetcar Named Desire* (NBT); *Ibi l'ohun* (Brest) and *God's Plenty* (Rambert). He will also be working on a new ballet for Ballet Gulbenkian. Opera: *Baa Baa Black Sheep* (Opera North); *Coronation of Poppea* (Japan); *Punch and Judy* (Aldeburgh, Berlin and Vienna) and *Il Trovatore* (Scottish Opera).

Kevin Walton Movement

Acting work ranges from classical texts to Live Art; including award-winning musicals and films such as Sam Mendes' productions of *Assassins* and *Cabaret*, Mike Leigh's *Topsy-Turvy* and productions for most of the UK's leading theatres. Kevin has a particular interest in physical and experimental theatre and has been a core member of devising ensembles such as the Medieval Players, the David Glass Ensemble, the Gary Carter Company and Lightwork.

He is Artistic Director of the visual music theatre ensemble LunaSea whose latest piece *The Moon Behind the Clouds* premiered recently at Battersea Arts Centre.

He has sung in classical opera houses in Italy, devised new work with Opera Circus and Impropera, he was also a founder member of Operaction, commissioned by London International Opera Festival to devise and produce new operas combining classical voices with circus and physical theatre skills. Recent solo recording work includes several albums with composer Jonathan Cooper and the award-winning soundtrack of the BAFTA nominated animation *Sap*.

Kevin is a visiting lecturer in performance at Central School of Speech and Drama and has also taught movement at both the University of Bristol and Goldsmith's College.

Jane Hytch Producer

Between 1980-1990 Jane set up and ran Worcester Arts Workshop, a community arts centre. The adventurous programme included producing a number of large-scale community plays in the style of Anne Jellicoe, most notably *Woodbine Willie* in 1985. This confirmed her commitment to working with local communities and individuals who for the most part have had little or no contact with theatre. In 1986/7 she designed and created numerous festivals and community processions, the largest scale one for Sandwell Community Arts – Community Fire Festival. In 1990 Jane set up Arts Exchange, a community group in Coventry, and then ran the community department at the Belgrade Theatre, producing two community plays for the Belgrade stage and numerous community-based theatre projects. In 1992 she set up Arts Alive, which became the largest festival of new theatre work in the West Midlands featuring the best local, national and international theatre. In 1997 she became Associate Producer for the Belgrade, and produced *Wakey! Wakey! – In Bed With Billy Cotton* by Richard Cameron. In 1998, she produced *The Wedding* by Kathi Leahy and in 1999 *Cool Water Murder* by Chris O'Connell and the original production of *The Twits* by David Wood. 1999 also saw Jane receiving the largest Millennium Award for *Millennium Mystery Plays*; she also won the largest A4E Award for the collaboration between the Belgrade and seven small-scale theatre companies, creating the Coventry Theatre Network.

Further Belgrade credits include: *Fantastic Mr Fox* by David Wood, *A Midsummer Night's Dream*, co-produced with The Shysters, *Rumplestiltskin* by Matthew Pegg, *Larkin With Women* by Ben Brown (in association with Richard Jordan Productions Ltd), *The Millennium Mysteries* with Teatr Biuro Podrozy, *The Mysteries 2003* with Macnas, and Box Dem (co-production with Frontline AV). Jane is creating and producing the events programme for the theatre in collaboration with Coventry City Council which includes *Rootz* with Frontline AV, *Coventry Belgrade Mela* with Coventry Asian Arts and Cultural Forum, Coventry Carnival and MAD UK.

ⓑelgrade theatre
coventry

The Belgrade Theatre was built in 1958 as part of the reconstruction of Coventry after World War II. It was named in honour of the gift of timber from the former Yugoslavia used to help reconstruct the city.

Holding 866 in its two-tier main auditorium, it remains one of the largest regional producing theatres in Britain.

The theatre has a long history of producing new writing with early Company members at the Belgrade including Trevor Nunn, John Gunter, Joan Plowright, Michael Crawford, Frank Finlay and Leonard Rossiter, with Arnold Wesker and David Turner among the new dramatists.

The Belgrade is also the home of the Theatre-in-Education (TIE) movement, and continues to pioneer new initiatives in this field as well as other community and outreach programmes. 2006 will see the opening of a new 250-300 seat second space and refurbishment of the existing listed building in which the theatre can expand the range of work it produces and invites to play Coventry.

Hamish Glen has led the theatre since 2003 and his artistic policy ensures a commitment to the production of more new drama, such as Head/Case, in the future.

belgrade theatre
coventry

Belgrade Theatre Staff List

Board of Directors
Chair **David Burbidge OBE DL**
Vice Chair **Sue Wilson**
John Blundell
John Clarke
Carol Malcolmson
Alistair Petterson
Peter Pinnell
Martin Ritchley
David Shortland
Tony Skipper

Management
Artistic Director **Hamish Glen**
Executive Director **Joanna Reid**

Finance
Head of Finance **Andrea Simpson**
Accounts Manager **Linda Alger**
Payroll Officer/Accounts Assistant
Nicola Boyle
Capital Project Accountant **Surjit Sandhu**

Administration
PA to the Chief Executive **Denise Duncombe**
PA to Executive Director **Angela Naylor**
Admin Officers **Christine Dimond, Liz Hunter**

Events
Producer **Jane Hytch**

Community and Education Company
Associate Director – Community Company
Justine Themen
Theatre Projects Officer **Linda Leech**
Youth Theatre Director **Jenny Evans**
Acting Out Project Manager **Jenny McDonald**
Community Company Administrator
Debbie Hewitt

Production
Head of Production **Tony Guest**
Company Stage Managers **Lianne Bruce, Steve Cressy**
Deputy Stage Managers **Jane Andrews, Sara Austin-Wells**
Assistant Stage Managers **Beatrice Maguire, Elizah Jackson**
Production Assistant **Rita Smith**
Head of Lighting/Sound **David Muir**

Deputy Chief Electrician **Glyn Edwards**
Assistant Electrician **Caroline Shirville**
Sound Operator **Chris Mock**
Head Prop Maker **Sherri Hazzard**
Head Scenic Artist **Laura O'Connell**
Deputy Scenic Artist **Sandra Field**
Head of Wardrobe **Margaret Lock**
Deputy Head of Wardrobe **Mandy Brown**
Wardrobe Assistant **Julie Morgan**

Marketing
Director of Marketing **Antony Flint**
Press & PR Officer **Ray Clenshaw**
Marketing Officer **Jess Thomas**
Marketing Assistants **Lori Ford, Angela Tamufor, Helen Tovey**
Box Office Manager **Eamonn Finnerty**
Box Office Sales Assistants **Linda Grimmett, Valerie Gunter, Christine Jackson, Kaye Moore**
Marketing Volunteers **Helen Arnold, Maureen Connoll, Joan Howard, Doris Webb**

Front of House
Theatre Manager **Jonathan Bainbridge**
Assistant Theatre Manager **Carol Tomlinson**
Front of House Manager **Margaret Rogers**
Duty House Manager (part-time) **Sue Smith**
Senior Usher and Duty Manager **Kate Copland**
Ushers **Lee Barnes, Sarah Benn, Eddie Brewster, Jennifer Chatfield, Lori Ford, Sheila Hart, Samantha Please, Doreen Smallman, Sandra Stockwin, Colin Turner, Dan Whitfield**
Housekeeper **Christina Ivens**
Cleaners **Moira Barker, Maureen Billings, Irene Cheston, Jackie Gardner, Wayne Gardner, Maureen Hicks, Barbara Thompson**
Senior Maintenance Officer **Paul Duncombe**
Maintenance Officer **David Eales**
Access Officer **Judith Ogden**
Audio Describers **Keith Bradbury, Jess Thomas, Will Wiltshire, Phil Woodcock**
Sign Language Interpreters **Clare Edwards, Anji Gregg, Rachel Tipping**

Catering
Catering Manager **Lynne Craig**
Head Chef/Deputy Catering Manager
Gavin Stevens
Catering Supervisors **Stacey Craig,
Christopher Pearce**
Catering Staff **Selina Braithwaite,
Michael Duffy, Clement Dupreneuf,
Mairetta Gallagher, Nell Jones, Charan
Kaur, Mindy Kaur, Michelle Mooney,
Joseph Sherriff, Glenn Sherlock**

Capital Development Scheme
Project Director **David Beidas**
Head of Fundraising **Jill Mowlam**
Project Manager **Buro Four**
Architect **Stanton Williams**
Structural Engineer **Flint and Neil**
Services Engineer **Rybka**
Theatre Consultant **Theatreplan**
Acoustics **Arup Acoustics**
Access Consultant **All Clear Designs**
Planning Supervisor **Quoin Consultancy**
Cost Consultant **Davis Langdon and
Everest**

Ron Hutchinson on Irish Identity

It was John Claypole's fist that first made me think about the question of national identity. One day after we moved from Belfast to Coventry he came to the back gate with some of his mates and asked if I was Irish. When I said yes he broke my nose with one punch – the (to me, remote) justification, I later learned, being Coventry's experience of IRA terrorism. Maybe I should have delayed before replying, for, being a Northern Irish Protestant I could have said I was an Irish asterisk – British Irish. Or maybe just British. Or allowed things to get really complicated by explaining that some of the Ulster Scots Irish would claim to be the real Irish, having been dispossessed originally by the Dublin Viking Irish who now claim to be the real Irish.

Very probably no answer parsing exactly what tribe I should claim to belong to would have been acceptable – my nose being too tempting a target. Today my answer might be even more confused – "I'm a Scots Irishman who spent many years in England, now married to a Roman Catholic New Yorker with Jewish and Russian roots, living in a Korean, Hispanic and African-American enclave in Los Angeles".

And yet, when asked where I come from, I say Ireland (even though my passport says the United Kingdom) and if asked what I am, I'd be inclined to say Irish (even though I haven't set foot there in fifteen years).

And you—? Where do you come from? And does that have any bearing on who you are? Think twice before you answer. Abstract question though it may seem, the issue of national identity can still add fist to nose…

Into The Silent Land

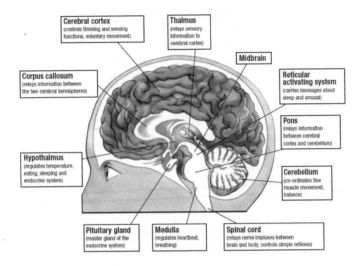

"Like the surface of the Earth, the brain is pretty much mapped. There are no secret compartments inaccessible to the surgeon's knife or the magnetic gaze of the brain scanner; no mysterious humours pervading the cerebral ventricles, no soul in the pineal gland, no vital spark, no spirits in the tangled wood. There is nothing you can't touch or squeeze, weigh and measure, as we might the physical properties of other objects. So you will search in vain for any semblance of a self within the structures of the brain: there is no ghost in the machine. It is time to grow up and accept this fact. But, somehow, we are the product of the operation of this machinery and its progress through the physical and social world.

Minds emerge from process and interaction, not substance. In a sense, we inhabit the spaces between things. We subsist in emptiness. A beautiful, liberating thought and nothing to be afraid of. The notion of tethered soul is crude by comparison. Shine a light, it's obvious."

This extract is taken from Into the Silent Land *by Paul Broks, published by Atlantic Books, an imprint of Grove Atlantic Ltd © Paul Broks 2003.*

Headway Bristol

Headway Bristol came into existence in 1977 as the result of families needing to talk to others who had been and were experiencing the trauma of their loved one having a head injury and often remaining in a coma for some weeks or even months and some who were never going to wake at all.

This resulted in families and carers supporting each other and passing on their knowledge to those who were experiencing the same trauma, bearing in mind that neurosurgeons were, and still are, unable to forecast outcomes after brain damage. It became well known that rehabilitation was almost non-existent in the early days and even now is scarce due to the tremendous cost over many years to the NHS. This resulted in families becoming determined to help themselves and Headway Bristol opened its headway house in 1989. In the early 1990s the families raised £250,000 to build a new Headway House, which is now situated in the grounds of Frenchay Hospital, a centre of excellence for neurosurgery. This Day unit is still very much a part of the rehabilitation process of young brain-damaged people and it provides social rehabilitation and stimulation.

This is good for the damaged brain and helps lift the low feelings of both the damaged person and their families or carers. Headway House staff and volunteers realise they cannot wave a magic wand to make people better but they can love them and help to recover as best they can. Fundraising is an important part of the Bristol Headway Group and at the moment they are endeavouring to raise sufficient funds to take those attending Headway House for a holiday next year. The idea is to take them on a holiday to France so they can feel they are able to travel abroad as other young people do who have not received brain damage.

Headway Bristol is very appreciative of the efforts being made on behalf of some wonderful people who are striving daily to improve and we thank everyone involved.

If you would like to make a donation, please make the cheque payable to Headway Bristol, and forward to Headway House, Frenchay Hospital, Frenchay Park Road, Bristol, BS16 1EH.

HEAD/CASE

First published in 2005 by Oberon Books Ltd
521 Caledonian Road, London N7 9RH
Tel: 020 7607 3637 / Fax: 020 7607 3629
e-mail: oberonbooks@btconnect.com
www.oberonbooks.com

A catalogue record for this book is available from the British
Library.

ISBN: 1 84002 540 9

Printed in Great Britain by Antony Rowe Ltd, Chippenham

The action takes place in a Halfway Home in which

TRACY

JULIA

and

JIMMY

are recovering from brain damage
caused by frontal lobe injury.

ACT ONE

When the lights rise TRACY is in full spate, a torrent of words spilling from her in a Belfast accent.

TRACY is wearing a name tag with T R A C Y spelled out in block capitals attached to an anorak pulled over a shapeless dress. She's wearing heavy hiking boots without the laces, her hair is disordered. She can't keep still for a moment; she rocks backwards and forwards or sways from side to side, her hands are always rubbing against each other or her body or diving in and out of the pockets on her skirt, she's constantly pulling out a small makeup mirror and staring into it, before pushing it back into her pocket.

TRACY: The thing is, you see, one of the things is, if I keep yakking, if I keep saying things, like, anything at all, the first thing that comes into my head, something like *See, if I keep yakking, if I keep saying things, anything at all, the first thing that comes into my head* – if I keep doing that – and maybe I'm doing it right now, right this minute, this very minute, maybe saying the first thing that comes into my head right now, here and now – well maybe that's because when I'm doing that I don't have to stop and think what I'm trying to say, what I *should* be saying, what the subject is, what the crack's meant to be about, if you know what I mean, *focus,* is that the word I'm looking for because if you keep yakking, I suppose, it means you don't lose track of whatever it is you're supposed to be focusing on and I can see that could be a problem if somebody had something happen to them, like what happened to me, like what they tell me *apparently* happened to because I'd have trouble keeping track, keeping on the rails, I'd be yakking and yakking and yakking and yakking and yakking and yakking and

yakking and yakking and yakking and yakking and
yakking and yakking and yakking and yakking and
yakking and yakking and yakking and yakking and
yakking and yakking and yakking and yakking and
yakking and yakking and yakking and yakking –

She giggles, gives a little skip in those heavy boots.

– and yakking and yakking and yakking but what I'd
really be hoping is that my brain somehow or other is
going to catch up with my gob so the main reason, and
now we're getting to it, the main reason – I think it's the
main reason anyhow – that I'd keep yakking and
yakking and yakking and yakking and yakking and
yakking and yakking and yakking is because I wouldn't
have to stop and think what I'm trying to say, what I
should be saying, what the crack's meant to be about, if
you know what I mean, *focus,* is that the word I'm
looking for? Or did I just say that? Was that me?
Because sometimes I say something and I forget I said it,
even if I just said it, because sometimes I say something
and I forget I said it, even if I just said it, because
sometimes I say something and I forget I said it, even if
I just said it –

She giggles, gives another little skip, checks herself in the mirror –

Okay, okay, okay, I'm talking too much, I know that –

She takes a small notebook out, opens it, reads –

Shut your mouth and give your arse a chance.

She giggles again, closes the book again –

I'm Tracy. I'm Irish.

She indicates the note on her lapel –

T-R-A-C-Y –

That's me. T-R-A-C-Y spells Tracy. Tracy is the name of
a person. C-H-A-I-R spells chair. You sit on a chair. A
chair is something you sit on. There are things and there
are things called words that tell you what those things
are. The word for the thing you sit on is chair. That's a
chair over there. You sit on a chair –

She moves to the chair, demonstrating –

Sit –

She sits, then springs to her feet again –

Sit –

She sits, then springs to her feet again –

Sit –

She sits, then springs to her feet again –

Sit –

She sits, then springs to her feet again –

Sit –

She sits, then springs to her feet again –

Sit –

She sits, then springs to her feet again –

Sit –

She sits, then springs to her feet again –

Sit –

She sits, then springs to her feet again –

Sit –

TRACY suddenly sits, instantly starts to squirm and rock from side to side, while rubbing her hands on her legs.

Something happened to me, I know that.

Without warning TRACY swats at the side of her head –

Eejit eejit eejit eejit eejit eejit eejit eejit eejit eejit eejit eejit eejit eejit –

She stops swatting –

Something happened –

TRACY shrugs, rocks from side to side, slumped in the chair, making humming noises in the back of her throat as she throws herself into a high speed monologue, hardly pausing for breath –

Some people have things happen to them that make it hard to get on with the real world because these people, who had this thing happen to them, these people wouldn't have what other people have, the Normies, what they take for granted, when they wake up every day and brush their teeth and wash their face and do their hair and put on their bras and knickers and skirts and shoes –

She stops abruptly, peers at her feet –

S-H-O-E-S. That spells shoes. You wear shoes. Shoes is the word for shoes. There is no other word for shoes. I am wearing shoes. The thing called a word for the things called shoes is shoes. Those are your shoes –

She rocks even more violently, rubs her hands on her legs even more frantically, pulling the mirror out, checking how she looks, putting it away again –

What I'm trying to say, what I think I'm trying to say, if I'm making any sense at all is that these people would have something taken from them, or at the very least they'd be *told* that something had been taken from them, they'd be trying to get these people to *understand* something had gone West and so these people, who had this thing happen to them, or the people you would have to keep *telling* had this thing happen to them because of course they'd be the last to know that, they'd have to start the job of making a new person out of what's left –

She's rocking backwards and forwards as well as from side to side now, making strange little noises in the back of her throat –

Because when you get a brain injury it wouldn't be like having a broken leg, would it? You've got a broken leg –

You get out of bed, you fall on the floor –

She topples to the floor from the chair –

Jesus – what was that? Oh I remember now, I broke my leg.

She giggles, looks down at her leg –

It's a broken leg, would you look at that, it's all coming back to me, bloody thing –

She scrambles to her feet again –

Can't see your brain though, can you? Eh? It's up there somewhere and you have to use your brain to think about your brain so if there's something wrong with it, you'd be the last person to find out, wouldn't you?

Wouldn't you? Wouldn't you? Wouldn't you? Wouldn't you? Wouldn't you? Wouldn't you? Wouldn't you? Wouldn't you?

TRACY giggles, checks how she looks in the mirror again.

The lights rise on JULIA, standing facing her, head cast down, slightly stooped. She's holding a small case. TRACY walks towards her.

When TRACY walks she swings her right arm with her right leg and vice versa, rolls her shoulders; now and again gives a little skip in her hiking boots and when she changes the direction in which she looks, has to swivel her whole body from the hips.

I'm Tracy. I'm Irish. T-R-A-C-Y. That spells Tracy. I-R-I-S-H spells Irish. Would you like to know how to sit? I could show you that. Yes? Yes yes yes yes yes yes yes yes yes yes yes yes yes yes yes yes yes yes yes yes yes yes yes?

She sits in the chair slumping in the chair, making random, restless movements, taking out the makeup mirror and checking how she looks.

This is not how you sit in a chair. No. No no no no no no no no no no no no. Oh no indeedy. They had to teach me to sit in a chair again, so they did, so I can show you. When you sit in a chair you sit like this –

TRACY pulls herself upright.

You take deep breaths, keep your mitts still, you sit upright – you do not sit like this –

TRACY's already starting to slump back again.

You sit like this –

TRACY hauls herself upright again but her knees are jogging and she's making noises in her throat.

Not like this –

Like this.

She tries to stop her knees jogging but her hands at once start to rub against her legs.

Not like this –

Like this –

TRACY's hands stop moving but her foot starts to tap.

Not like this –

Like this.

TRACY's foot stops tapping but her head's nodding from side to side.

Not like this –

Like this.

TRACY's head stop moving but she's making noises in her throat.

Not like this –

Like this.

The noises stop but now TRACY's crossing and uncrossing her legs.

Not like this –

Like this.

With a huge effort TRACY forces herself to sit stock still for a second. Then she starts to sway violently backwards and forwards, sometimes reaching down to hug her ankles, then pull herself upright again –

Uh oh –

She makes herself stop rocking –

This is me trying to sit like a normal person, like somebody who isn't an eejit or a little girl, I am not a little girl, I'm thirty-five years old and there are some things I can do and some things I can't do and being five years old again, isn't one of them, or six or seven or eight or nine or ten –

Without realizing, she starts rocking again –

Grown up people don't rock from side to side when they're sitting down and they know what to do with their hands, so they do –

She giggles, clasps them again, stops rocking –

This is how a thirty-five year old woman sits – she doesn't rock from side to side like an eejit and she doesn't rub her hands up and down on her legs like an eejit.

She forces herself to sit upright, hands clasped again.

She holds the position for a moment, then giggles again, gets to her feet, indicates the case still in JULIA's hand –

Would you ever put that down?

JULIA: The case?

TRACY: The case.

JULIA's voice is flat, uninflected. When she moves it's in total contrast to TRACY's sudden, awkward strides and gestures.

JULIA hesitates, then sets the case down.

TRACY leans forward, suddenly intent, struggling to focus –

Trying to say trying to say trying to say trying to say –

With a huge effort she screws up her face in concentration –

There's *something* not right with me, I know that, I've got the engine and the gears and the accelerator but I don't have the brake, you might say, one might say, *it could be said,* so one of the things I'm here to learn, *apparently,* is how to stop myself yakking and yakking and yakking and yakking and yakking and yakking and yakking and yakking and yakking when I'm yakking just for the sake of it, yakking and yakking and yakking and yakking and yakking and yakking because when I'm yakking I don't feel scared or depressed or remember I'm not normal and when I'm making an arse of meself it's the same thing, *apparently, it could be said,* acting like a bigger eejit than I really even am, which is saying something –

She rocks backwards and forwards, stops herself with a great effort.

I know it's because I've got this sick head, I've got this sick thinking –

She swats forlornly at the side of her head again –

Sick sick sick sick sick sick sick sick sick –

She stop swatting –

Or *apparently* I do, because something happened that I can't remember, that they *tell me* happened, although I've

27

no way of knowing one way or the other so I have to take it on trust that really was me, *apparently* was me, *they say it was* and that has to be good enough –

Hastily –

And I'm not saying they're wrong because I know I'm not right up here, I know there's a screw and a couple of bolts loose somewhere because if there wasn't why would I be here? Why would you be here? Because we've got holes in our heads and the thing about having a hole in your head is that –

Getting animated again, TRACY giggles and pulls out the notepad and pencil.

    Wash hair.

She writes the words down, tears the sheet out of the pad –

    The thing is – to remember to read it I've got to –

She writes the words on another sheet –

    Read note about hair.

She tears that sheet of paper off the pad.

    Hang on –

She writes again –

    Read note about reading note about hair.

She tears that sheet off.

    Hang on –

She writes again –

Read note about reading note about reading note about hair.

She tears that sheet off.

Hang on –

She writes again –

Read note about reading note about reading note about reading note about hair.

She tears that sheet off.

Hang on –

She writes again –

Read note about reading note about reading note about reading note about hair.

Giggling, manic again, she pulls more pages out of the pad –

And on and on and on and on and on and on and on and on and on and on and on and on and on and on –

You see where I'm going? You see the problem? The problemo? Do you have that problem too?

She puts the pad and pencil away again –

Sure it's nothing to be ashamed of, having a sick head, having a hole in your head, daylight between your ears, shit for brains, we can't help what's happened to us or what they *tell us* happened to us, it's just we have a hard time doing some of the things that normal people do, people who do not keep yakking and yakking, in my case, saying the first thing that comes into their heads or in your case not saying the first thing that doesn't comes into your head or anything at all, The Human Clam, but the great thing is not to panic when it doesn't seem to make sense because I stopped a brick or that's what they tell me. You?

JULIA: Yes?

TRACY: What happened to you?

JULIA: Oh –

TRACY: I'm Irish.

She shrugs. TRACY pulls out the mirror, sneaks a covert look at herself again –

I didn't look like this before. But this is me, now. Since I got hit by a brick. You? Did you get hit by a brick?

JULIA: I don't –

She shrugs.

TRACY: I don't remember, either. But that's what they tell me. Head. Brick. That was it. You?

JULIA: I don't –

She shrugs again. TRACY looks in the mirror again –

TRACY: It's hard to keep the weight off. No control, you see. Since I got hit by a brick. You?

JULIA: I don't –

She shrugs.

TRACY: Nor me. But that's why I act like a big kid. A kid with a bucket for a brain. A bucket with a hole in it. You?

JULIA: I don't –

She shrugs.

TRACY: I'll never get it back, not all of it. What I had
when I got hit by a brick. You?

*JULIA concentrates. When she starts to speak it's as if she's breaking
a silence that has lasted for centuries; she fights for each word, at
every moment has to stop herself from subsiding into passivity, let
herself remain mired in her condition. She's fighting, too. It's not
such a spectacular fight as TRACY's but just as intense.*

JULIA: I was in my car one day…and I dropped something
on the…floor and I bent to pick it up and…this all
happened to…somebody else, of course, not to me…
there was *somebody* who was in her…car one day and took
her seat belt off and just then…somebody else ran into
her car…not me…because I don't remember it…she was
in her car and her…seat belt was off and another
car…not going all that fast…not really…ran into
her…and she banged her head and…and that was the end
of her…

TRACY's been jiggling her foot, as if impatient to get speaking again –

TRACY: Hm hm hm hm hm hm hm hm hm – (*Abruptly.*)
Are you scared of me?

JULIA: I don't –

TRACY: People *are* scared of me. I've been a bad girl
before now –

TRACY takes out the mirror, stares at herself –

A bad bad bad bad bad bad bad bad bad bad bad bad
bad bad bad bad bad bad girl – (*Grins.*) I bite people. I
hit them.

Bad bad bad bad bad bad bad bad –

She puts the mirror away, guiltily –

I shouldn't do that with the mirror. That's one of the things I'm working on.

She pulls her notebook out –

It's here, see – about the mirror. It stops me focussing and that's a bad thing. Of course stopping a brick is a bad thing. That's what happened to me. You? Oh, the car, yeah.

TRACY's hand steals to the mirror again. She stares at herself in it, holding it inches from her face.

Would a reflection in a mirror know that it was a reflection? What do you think? It'd think it was real, wouldn't it? You're looking at it and it's looking back at you while you're looking at it while it's looking back at you while you're looking at it while it's looking back at you and you're thinking *sure this is me here* and it's maybe thinking *no, this is me here* while you're thinking *sure, this is me here* while it's maybe thinking *no, this is me here* –

She looks up suddenly, puts the mirror back into her anorak –

Would you like a hand with that?

She indicates the suitcase.

JULIA: They sent me here I suppose because…nothing really…mattered after the car…there wasn't anything it was…worth paying any attention to…nothing to get… interested in…

…like…coming up from the bottom of the sea… coming…out of the coma but I never…made it all the way…I got stuck somewhere…and I'm still…still stuck…

TRACY takes the suitcase, starts to unpack the items inside it – a change of clothes, nightdress, toiletries.

TRACY: When I got hit by a brick it damaged something called the frontal lobe. I'm told. The frontal lobe is what helps us control our impulses. I'm told.

JULIA: (*The suitcase.*) I'll do that –

TRACY: (*Ignores her.*) I can't do that automatically any more. I have to do it by asking myself, every minute of the day, is what I'm doing appropriate? Appropriate to a thirty-five year old woman and not a five year old with a bucket for a head and a bucket with a hole in it.

JULIA: I'll do that –

TRACY: Or that's what they tell me, why they put me here because disinhibition, okay, it's like – only I'm not supposed to say *what it's like,* I'm supposed to just say *what it is* because that's supposed to help me deal with it, keeping my focus, my hocus pocus – what it means is, like, when somebody, has my kind of brain injury – but that's not right either –

JULIA: I'll do that –

TRACY: – because when you're trying to tell somebody something like *what is disinhibition?* – you should say it right away and not be beating about the bush, here we go round the or say you don't understand it and not keep yakking and yakking and yakking just to keep saying something, when you're trying to tell somebody what

Disinhibition is – dis-in-e-what? – Disinhibition, you see, is – dis-in-e-what? –

She swats her head –

Stupid head stupid head, stupid stupid head –

She stops hitting her head as JULIA goes to the suitcase to retrieve her possessions –

Did they tell you you were going to get better? I'm not. Not better like I was before. I've had a bit taken away from me, you see, I'm never going to get back. But it does mean sometimes I can't help asking what's the point? Did they tell you –? (*The suitcase.*) I'll do that –

Did they tell you that – did they tell you anything – is there any point them telling you anything? – to take one day at a time. But what I keep asking is who was I? Not the job I did, that's not what I mean what I mean what I mean what I mean – was I smart? Was I funny? Was I a bobby dazzler? But not even that's it –

She takes the suitcase from JULIA –

I said I'll do that –

What I mean what I mean what I mean what I mean what I mean –

What was I *like? Me?* Who was I? To *know?*

But they can't tell you that, can they? That's gone. There's no way of getting that back, for me *or* you.

JULIA: I don't –

TRACY: And don't say you don't. Don't don't don't don't don't don't don't don't. Don't what? What what what what what what what what what? You don't what?

JULIA: I don't know.

TRACY: Aren't I telling you? You're you but you're not you, not any more, like I'm me and not me, not like I was. What you want to be is her, I bet –

She pulls a framed photo of JULIA out of the case –

But you can't be her. Ever again.

JULIA reaches for the photo, TRACY pulls it away from her –

So that's one bet you lost. You're stuck with that like I'm stuck with –

She frames her head, as if she's in a photo frame –

So the great thing is not to fool yourself while you're here. Not to –

She mimes how JULIA stands and replies –

I don't –

She shrugs, as JULIA does, head down, face impassive.

I don't –

She shrugs, as JULIA does, head down, face impassive.

I don't –

She shrugs, as JULIA does, head down, face impassive.

I don't –

She shrugs, as JULIA does, head down, face impassive.

I don't –

She shrugs, as JULIA does, head down, face impassive.

Because you *do* – you have to.

JULIA: Okay.

TRACY: Okay?

JULIA: Okay.

TRACY: Okay?

JULIA: Okay.

TRACY: Okay?

JULIA: Okay.

TRACY: Okay?

JULIA: Okay.

TRACY: What do you mean, okay?

JULIA: I mean –

She shrugs again.

TRACY: You should be scared of me.

JULIA: I don't –

TRACY: Do you think I'm an eejit?

JULIA: I didn't –

TRACY: You want to be careful how you talk to me.

TRACY plants herself in front of her, challenging and physically confrontational –

You know how you talk to eejits? You look them in the eye and you put on this *Hallo, I'm talking to an eejit* voice –

She mimics JULIA's level, calm delivery –

That's how they talk to you here. They're highly trained in the care and treatment of eejits and looking at you with their *this is how you look at an eejit* look. They have to look the eejits in the eye and keep their voice like this because it's the only thing that works, you can't talk to us like you'd talk to a normal person, we're all a couple of spanners short of a toolbox after all – but maybe, just maybe if the eejit they're dealing with learns how to sit up straight and walk into a room right nobody will notice she's an eejit, she'll be able to get out there, in the real world and nobody'll be any the wiser – but of course the poor cow's always going to be as big an eejit as she was the day she walked into the brick or got hit by a car, was it? – but with any luck you'd never know the wind still whistles through the hole in her head.

She skips, giggles –

And I need to pee –

She hoists up her skirts, squats. JIMMY enters through the door. JULIA moves between them, sits, upstage.

JIMMY: Is that how a normal person behaves? Is it?
Scaring yon poor wee girl. The minute she gets here.

He mimes how she's walking –

Or is it – *I'm Tracy, I'm thirty-five years old and I'm an eejit* –

He sticks his hand out in a stiff handshake –

How do you do? How are you? How nice to see you. Can I pee on your floor? (*Tuts.*) Bad girl. Bad girl. Bad bad bad bad bad.

Who's been a bad girl then? Who's been a bad girl? Who's been a bad bad bad bad bad bad bad bad girl? Peeing on the floor is a bad thing to do, normal people do not do that, that is something only an eejit would do – how many times do I have to tell you?

Look how you're holding yourself –

He gently corrects her stance –

A normal person doesn't stare straight ahead, remember? – scaring the life out of you, she looks around the room and says *hello* to people, she makes eye contact *how are you doing, nice to see you, can I pee on your floor?* No, she doesn't do that, wrong answer – she looks around like this, she makes *eye contact* –

He mimics a normal person entering a room –

It's hard for you, I know, I know, because you don't see too good out of your right eye, your right eye's the wrong eye, your left eye's your right eye, if you see what I mean –

He moves her hands alternately over her eyes –

Left right left right left right left right left right left right left right left right left right so when Tracy wants to look at you Tracy has to turn her whole body, which makes her look like an eejit which isn't what we're after, is it?

He gently demonstrates, turning her entire body around first one way, then another –

Normal people do not do that, do they? –

TRACY: But I'm not, am I? I'm not normal. I'm never going to be a normal person again, I'm maybe never going to be any kind of a person again –

JIMMY: Unless you work at it, unless you do the work –

TRACY: But I don't know there's anybody there, do I? That there really is somebody called Tracy there.

TRACY has taken out the mirror and is staring at herself –

JIMMY: Put that away and stop acting like an eejit.

TRACY: That's what I am.

TRACY pulls away from him, kicks off her boots, throws her anorak on the floor, starts writing her name over and over on slips of paper, sticking them all over her clothes.

JIMMY: No you're not. My cousin Paddy is. The Dole sends him for a job on a building site. The Foreman says *With all this Health and Safety Stuff we have to be very careful. There's a lot of complicated machinery like hammers lying around on a site. I'll have to give you an IQ test but I'll go easy on you. What's got four fingers, one thumb and is made of wool or leather?*

That's a tough one, says Paddy. *Could you give us a clue?*

It's a glove, says the Foreman.

Of course it is, says Paddy. *It was on the tip of me tongue. Give me another.*

What's got eight fingers and two thumbs and is made of wool or leather?

Jaysus, says Paddy, *you've got me beat again.*

It's two gloves.

God Almighty, says Paddy, *how'd I miss that?*

Your third and final question, says the Foreman. *What country is the Queen of England the Queen of?*

Paddy thinks for a minute – *Is it three gloves?*

TRACY is still slapping the pieces of paper on her clothes –

Now that's an eejit. Like me other cousin Mick. He's lost in the desert. He finds this little teapot and gives it a rub with his elbow and this fucking great genie appears. *I am the Genie of the Lamp,* he says, *you have three wishes, pal.*

I'm dying for a drink, says Mick. *Could I have a never-ending bottle of Guinness? Your wish is my command,* says the Genie, and there's a blue flash and there's an ice cold bottle of stout in your man's hand. He knocks it back, empties it in one go, holds it up to the light and sure enough – it fills up again.

Good God almighty, says Mick. *I'll have two more of these.*

That's an eejit. The kind of eejit who won't go into a paper shop in case it blows away. Who's got three books on the shelf – *Who's Who, Who's That* and *That's Him.*

That's not you, is it? That's not Tracy. All Tracy needs is to stop making herself the centre of attention all the time. It's very simple. It's not doing the stuff that makes people maybe *think* she's an eejit –

It's not – what?

TRACY: Not stuffing herself until she's bursting and still keeping eating?

JIMMY: Not –

TRACY: Acting the goat?

JIMMY: Not –

TRACY: Having other people scared of being around you?

JIMMY: Not –

TRACY: Playing with yourself when you shouldn't?

JIMMY: Not –

TRACY: Knowing you're making an arse of yourself and not being able to stop it?

JIMMY: Not –

TRACY: Being able to go anywhere because you're not welcome?

JIMMY: Not –

TRACY: Taking a swing at someone when you're mad at them?

JIMMY: Not –

TRACY: Biting people? Not spitting at them? Not giving them a shove instead of asking them to get out of your way? Not wanting your own way all the time and not seeing why you can't have it? Not wanting to stop being an eejit but not being able to?

JIMMY: And one hundred per cent it's not what?

TRACY: Peeing on somebody's floor? Is that what she did? Just now?

TRACY points to one of the labels –

Tracy –?

She points to the others, all over her body –

Tracy Tracy Tracy Tracy Tracy Tracy Tracy Tracy Tracy Tracy Tracy Tracy –? Did she do that?

She takes one off, turns, bends over, slaps it on her backside –

Tracy –? (*Abruptly.*) I'm Irish and I got hit by a brick, did you know that?

JIMMY: Yes.

TRACY: It knocked most of me brains out.

JIMMY: I know.

TRACY: I'll never be right again.

JIMMY: Remember what they told you when they put you here. You have a chance to do something very few people do. You have the chance to start all over and make a new person. And maybe you could get to like that person just as well, or better.

TRACY: But I keep making an arse of myself.

JIMMY: You do, yes.

TRACY: Like just now.

JIMMY: You let yourself down again, I know.

TRACY: Why do you stay with me?

JIMMY: Don't start on that bloody tune again.

TRACY: Did you love me? Before? For who I was? Then?

JIMMY: Ah shut your mouth and give your arse a chance.

TRACY: But you say you love me now. *This.*

JIMMY: I do, so I do.

TRACY: They're different people.

JIMMY: The same to me. Sure you were always a bit of a pain in the crack at times – like you're being now.

TRACY: Won't you always be wanting *her* back?

JIMMY: You're still you.

TRACY: I'm not. I'm never going to be.

JIMMY: Did you hit her?

TRACY: No.

JIMMY: Did you bite her?

TRACY: No.

JIMMY: You're sure?

TRACY: I just –

She mimes squatting again.

JIMMY: Dirty cat.

TRACY: There's just this big stone English face taking a screw at you – (*Miming JULIA.*) *I don't* – I had to do *something*.

JIMMY: To take a rise out of her?

TRACY: Yes.

JIMMY: Take a hand out of her?

TRACY: Yes.

JIMMY: By peeing on her floor?

TRACY: You're not mad at me? Making an arse of meself again?

JIMMY: I'd be proud of you, whatever.

TRACY: Even though I've got a sick head?

JIMMY: Sure who hasn't?

TRACY: Even though I'm a big eejit?

JIMMY: Who isn't?

He holds her hands, does a little waltz step with her, ignoring her clumsy, awkward feet –

> *When first I saw the lovelight in your eyes*
> *I thought the world held naught but joy for me*
> *And even though we drifted far apart*

I never dreamed but what I dream of thee –

She squints suspiciously at him –

TRACY: You're not mad at me? You're sure?

JIMMY: No.

TRACY: Would you ever get mad at me?

JIMMY: (*Sings, ignoring it.*) *I love you as I never loved before –*

TRACY: Whatever I did?

JIMMY: *Since first I saw you on the village green –*

TRACY: If I keep making an arse of meself.

JIMMY: *Come to me or my dream of love is o'er –*

TRACY: Since I got hit by a brick?

JIMMY: *I love you as I loved you –*

TRACY: Which I don't remember.

JIMMY: *When you were sweet sixteen –*

He pulls away from her –

Can you do better this time? Can you?

TRACY heads stage right as the lights dim on JIMMY stage left. She pulls the chair so closer to JULIA their knees are almost touching. JULIA stares impassively back at her. TRACY tries to force herself to sit still. It takes a tremendous effort but she manages it. She holds it for a moment only before she slumps again. She reaches for the mirror, them pushes it away again. She sounds subdued, almost scared.

TRACY: I'm trying. I really am trying.

TRACY reaches for the makeup mirror, but pulls her hand away even before she can pull it out.

It's two steps back for every step forward, I know. But I try. I do try.

TRACY is grimacing with the effort of sitting upright and still.

I don't want to be like this. Different. I want to be the same as everybody else.

Her voice sounds despairing.

I do I do I do I do I do I do I do I do I do I do I do I do I do I do I do I do, I don't want to be an eejit the rest of me life, an eejit, an eejit, look at the eejit, would you take a look at her, the big eejit, I don't want them to look at me in the street, I don't want you to be scared of me –

JULIA: I'm not –

She shrugs.

TRACY: But if you are –

JULIA: I'm –

She shrugs.

TRACY: I peed on your floor.

JULIA: I know.

TRACY: How could you not be angry?

JULIA: It's –

She shrugs.

TRACY: You're not?

JULIA: I don't –

TRACY: Don't start that again.

Do you ever get angry? About anything?

JULIA: I think I –

She shrugs. TRACY leans forward.

TRACY: What's it like, in there, for you?

JULIA: Oh –

TRACY: No, what's it *like?*

JULIA makes the greatest effort she's made so far –

JULIA: I'm in the…hospital…watching the…television. I
don't…want to, it hurts my…ears, it's always too…
loud…they put…me in front of it every afternoon…
hours at a time…later they tell me it's a way to…
stimulate my… up here, keep it working, responding…
but I think it was just to put me somewhere, without
having…to deal…with me…people hold up things in
front of me when they pass my…bed…say *this is a comb,
this is a brush, this is a book, this is a key* and wait…for me
to say the word they've just said, which takes a long
time, saying something…doing anything takes a long
long time, I have to drag it out of some deep deep…
tunnel…and it's easier not…to say anything at all…

It seems more…important to…them than to me but…if I
think for…I don't know …weeks or months or years…I
might get the answer…I don't mind…if it's years…that's

how long anything…takes…years and years and years…
just reaching for something on the…bedside table…

JULIA hunches forward, forcing the words out, forcing herself to stay interested enough to say them –

When I reach…

She puts her arm out, holding it in the air –

It takes so long…and by the time it gets there…I've
forgotten what I'm reaching for…because…why?…I
mean…why bother? …because I was in my car one
day…and I dropped something on the…floor and I bent
to pick it up and…this all happened to…somebody else,
of course, not to me…and…somebody ran into her car…
not me…because I don't remember it…and she banged
her head and…and that was the end of her…

TRACY: You don't get angry?

JULIA: I hear…angry…I hear…I should be angry but…for
me…in here…it's like I'm…standing on the platform and
watching…everybody inside the train…talking and
laughing and waving and –

She silently mouths words –

And sometimes I –

She lifts her hand in a wave –

Because it seems to make them…feel better…but I don't
really care…there's nothing to…care about…but just to
keep them happy, because they seem to expect it…so
once in a while I…

She waves again –

And I…

She puts on a dazzling smile –

Because they like that, too…but I don't *know* angry…I don't know *to feel…*

TRACY: I'm sick of it. I am so sick of it. Sick of the whole shooting match. Sick sick sick sick sick sick sick sick sick sick sick of it. Had it up to here. Here here here here here here here here.

JULIA: You see I…I got stuck somewhere…and I'm still… still stuck…

TRACY: I can't tell you I'm sorry I did it. Because it wasn't *me*. Well it was. But it wasn't. I have this problem controlling my impulses. But if you like I'll tell you I was. Sorry. I did it. If it makes you feel better?

JULIA: That's –

TRACY: You're sure?

JULIA: Yes.

TRACY: I can't say I won't do it again. Well I could but I'd be lying. I'll try. It's one of the things I'm here to do. Learn what you can do and what you can't do. Like sitting up straight –

She forces herself upright in the chair again –

Keeping your hands and legs still and not looking around like an eejit –

She mimes how she usually sits, giggles.

I've got a fella.

JULIA: Yes?

TRACY: In here.

JULIA: Yes?

TRACY: In my room.

JULIA: Yes?

TRACY: He's Irish. I'm Irish, did you know that?

TRACY pulls out the mirror –

What I want to know, what the question is, is say we get rid of this eejit here, this fat pig, shit for brains, this fat cow, say we get her out of the door and there's this other Tracy, who can live with other people without peeing on their floors, say she –

She indicates an invisible person entering the room –

Say that's her –

She pulls the mirror out –

One day. Would she be Irish, too?

JULIA: I don't –

TRACY: Would she?

JULIA: I don't –

TRACY: But would she?

JULIA takes a deep breath, as if about to launch herself into a statement, then subsides again.

And how would she know? Do you see what I mean?
What I mean, what I mean?

She rocks backwards and forwards, frustrated at not being able to find the words –

Do you see what I'm asking what I'm asking?

She forces herself to stop rocking –

There *was* a Tracy but she stopped a brick so forget
about her –

She gestures at her body –

And *this* isn't Tracy, right? – not yet, we're getting rid of
her, don't let the door handle catch you on the arse on
the way out –

She giggles, makes an effort to control herself –

One day there's going to be a new Tracy, that's what I'm
working on, like you're working on a new –

JULIA: Julia –

TRACY: But the thing is what I'm asking is, the thing is,
there's something that's not going to change, isn't there,
something I'm never going to get away from –

She beats her hands on her knees in frustration at not finding the words –

Trying to say trying to say trying to say trying to say –

Do you like the Irish?

JULIA: I...

TRACY: You're English, right?

JULIA: I…

TRACY: No, you *are*. And you *know* you are.

JULIA: Yes.

TRACY: *How* do you know? What's that feel like?

JULIA: I'm not…

TRACY: Oh I'm not saying you get up in the morning and it's *teeth, face, shoes,* BE ENGLISH but it is in a way, isn't it?

JULIA: I know I'm English, yes –

TRACY: *How* do you know?

JULIA: I do.

TRACY: Is that good enough?

JULIA: I don't –

TRACY: (*Getting frustrated.*) Trying to say trying to say trying to say –

I'd be Irish now, right. This minute. And you'd know that.

JULIA: The accent?

TRACY: If you couldn't hear that, would you still know, would there be something about me that told you?

JULIA: I –

TRACY: You're sure?

JULIA: Perhaps there –

TRACY: But there might be?

JULIA: Yes.

TRACY: What would that be?

JULIA: Words?

TRACY: Like?

JULIA: I don't –

TRACY: Like what?

JULIA: *Eejits.*

TRACY: You wouldn't say that?

JULIA: No.

TRACY: If I didn't say *eejits* –

JULIA: Could I –

TRACY: Could you tell?

JULIA: I'm not –

TRACY: It wouldn't be like talking to somebody who was English, would it?

JULIA: I'm –

TRACY: (*Stubborn.*) There'd be a difference? Wouldn't there? You'd know. And I'd know, too.

JULIA: So –

TRACY: So? You're an eejit, I'm an eejit. You're an *English* eejit, I'm an *Irish* eejit. But how do we know that? Inside? Because we do.

JULIA: If you –

TRACY: I do say.

JULIA: Why are you –?

TRACY: Trouble?

JULIA: I didn't –

JULIA gets up but TRACY heads for her, stands nose to nose with her –

TRACY: They're trouble, aren't they?

JULIA: I didn't say –

TRACY: The Irish.

JULIA: Not –

TRACY: Not all?

JULIA: No –

JULIA tries to move around her but TRACY blocks her path –

TRACY: Some are more trouble than others?

JULIA: I –

TRACY does the impatient little dance again –

TRACY: Trying to say trying to say trying to say trying to say trying to say –

You might be on the lookout? For the Irish?

JULIA: No.

TRACY: (*Insistent.*) They'd be trouble.

JULIA: Not –

TRACY: The chances'd be me being more trouble than somebody else. Wouldn't they?

JULIA: Not –

TRACY: They're known for it. When you heard me open my eejit's gob, you *knew*. The first time I –

She slaps the side of her head, miming how she used to act –

Eejit eejit eejit eejit eejit –

She balls her fist –

You went *the Irish?*

JULIA: I –

TRACY: THE IRISH AGAIN.

JULIA: Maybe –

TRACY: You were scared of me?

JULIA: I –

TRACY: On your guard?

JULIA: I –

TRACY: Your back was up?

JULIA: It –

TRACY: Are you scared of me now?

JULIA: I –

JULIA moves but TRACY again stops her leaving –

TRACY: I don't understand *consequences*, you see. One of the things that goes with getting hit by a brick is I don't connect the dots. I have a hard job getting from where I am to where I want to be. That makes me angry. When I get angry I can't control my impulses because the bit of me bonce that did that got all fucked up. But it wasn't me that got angry. But it was. And I'm sorry. I'm sorry I did it. But I didn't. I take the blame. But I can't. And I wish I hadn't but I didn't. I won't do it again but I might. Julia? Is that your name?

She strides stage left, where JIMMY is waiting for her, sitting on the back of a chair. JULIA waits, impassive, stage right as TRACY kicks off her boots, pulls off her anorak, drops it on the floor, still marching around and swinging her arms.

She snatches a large container of ice cream from JIMMY's hand, starts to eat frantically, shovelling it into her mouth with a spoon, hardly stopping to breathe.

JIMMY: So it's Christmas Eve and Old Ma Riley's just got a quid for Christmas dinner. The butcher says *You can't get a turkey for that, love, but I've got a rabbit here.*

Go on, then, she says. He skins it and she puts it in her shawl but she's in such a hurry to get home she trips and it goes flying on the pavement.

Ah Jaysus. She bursts into tears and she's on her hands and knees crying her eyes out when the quare one leaves the pub and sees her. *Aw don't carry on, missis,* he says – *sure look at its ears – if it had lived it'd have been an eejit.*

I take it back. God love you, you are an eejit. You nearly hit her.

TRACY: No.

JIMMY: Yes.

TRACY: No.

JIMMY: Yes.

TRACY: I didn't.

JIMMY: You did.

TRACY: No.

JIMMY: Yes.

TRACY: No.

JIMMY: A poke in the jaw.

TRACY: No.

JIMMY: A smack in the gob.

TRACY: Yes.

JIMMY: There you are.

She hunches forward, obsessive, asks the same question she asked JULIA –

TRACY: What's it like? For you? In there?

JIMMY: In there?

TRACY: Up here –

Her fingers go to her head.

Inside?

JIMMY: I'm in the…bar…I'm reaching for a…a pint –

He mocks how JULIA reached her hand out –

It takes…takes so long and by the…the time it gets there I…I…I have…I have to go for a…a pee –

He grins –

I'm waiting…for a…train but all these…people inside it are…looking at me and…and saying…*look at that big fucking eejit…it's a bus stop.*

TRACY looks panicked suddenly –

TRACY: What'll I do?

JIMMY: Is it too hard?

TRACY: What'll I do?

JIMMY: What if I've had it?

TRACY: What'll I do?

JIMMY: What if that's it, this time, Goodnight Vienna?

TRACY: What if it's too hard?

JIMMY: What'll you do?

TRACY: What'll I do, what'll I do, what'll I do, what'll I do? I'm sick of it, sick of it, sick of it –

JIMMY: *You're* sick of it?

She keeps frantically eating as JIMMY stands over her, keeps repeating Sick of it *as she eats.*

I met this pal of mine. I says, *What are you doing now?*

He says, *I'm keeping bees.*

Away on, I says. *Bees, is it?*

Bees. No work, bags of honey.

Now how many bees would you get in an average hive? I ask him.

He says, *About a hundred – but I put a thousand in.*

A thousand? I says. *Don't they get all crushed?*

Sure they do, he says – *but fuck 'em.* (*Shrugs.*) Fuck 'em. What do you care. You could jump off a bridge, but where would be the imagination in that? Or step in front of a bus or a train and you lying there with your knickers showing –

Dignity would be important, convenience should never be overlooked, something easy to come to hand, something of a domestic nature, easily concealed from prying eyes, the accidental discovery –

He watches her still gulping down the ice cream –

Or you could stuff yourself with Raspberry Ripple till you burst. Have a titter of wit. Catch yourself on.

He indicates a bottle of pills being flown in –

A handful of these –

A bottle of Jameson whiskey flies in –

And a gargle of this – you're in clover.

He takes the pill box, unscrews the cap, holds a pill up to the light –

Now with yon, the timing's yours, not some Wally's
behind a wheel –

He takes the whiskey, takes the cap off the bottle, sniffs –

I'm a Bushmills man myself but –

*She puts the spoon down, stares at the pill and the bottle, ice cream
slathered on her face.*

Look at you –

He wipes the ice cream from her mouth and chin, singing –

*Near Banbridge Town
In the County Down
One morning last July
Down a boithrin green
Came a sweet colleen
And she smiled as she passed me by.*

She swallows the first pill, takes a drink of whiskey –

*She looked so neat
From her two bare feet
To the sheen of her nut-brown hair
Such a coaxing elf
Sure I shook meself
To make sure she was standing there –*

As the song continues he feeds her the pills and whiskey, ever faster –

From Bantry Bay

To the Derry Quay
And from Galway to Dublin Town
No maid I've seen
Like the brown colleen
That I met in the County Down –
And she onward sped
Sure I turned my head
And I gazed with a feeling rare
And I says, says I,
To a passer by
Who's the maid with the nut brown hair?
He smiled at me
And he says, says he,
'That's the gem of old Ireland's crown.
Sweet Rosie McCann
From the banks of the Bann
She's the Star of the County Down'

The pills and whiskey are disappearing even faster than ever –

From Bantry Bay
To the Derry Quay
And from Galway to Dublin Town
No maid I've seen
Like the brown colleen
That I met in the County Down –

JULIA enters, watches as TRACY swallows the pills, drinks. She doesn't do anything to help.

She'd a soft brown eye
And a look so sly
And a smile like the rose in June
And you hung on each note
From her lily white throat
As she lilted an Irish tune.
At the pattern dance

You were held in a trance
As she tripped through a reel or a jig
And when her eyes she'd roll
She'd coax, on my soul,
A spud from a hungry pig –

TRACY: Not –

Suddenly TRACY gets to her feet, swaying from side to side.

No – not – no –

She hurls the pills into the air, turns to JULIA, shaking –

I know I'm in the Halfway Home. By myself. Although I'm not. Although I am. Because he's here. But he's not. And I'm scared. I'm so, so scared…

The lights fade as we –

end Act One

ACT TWO

Minutes or hours or days later, TRACY's with JULIA. JIMMY can be seen, lounging on the bed at the rear of the stage, as if in another flat.

TRACY: But he *is* here. With me. In my flat. Up there. By ourselves. At the same time. That he isn't. In a flat that isn't there. But it is. Making a life for ourselves. Him and me. Though there's only me. Because he loves me. And I love him. Though I know he's not there, not really. But he is. Just like you're there. But he's not. Or is he?

I could tell you what he's wearing now.

Jeans, shirt, brown shoes, brown hair; we're engaged but we haven't really talked about the wedding yet though we have and it's going to be this June but it's not and I know what he does but I don't because he's not there, not really but he is, I can tell you the colour of his car, what side of the bed he sleeps on, how he likes his eggs, what he reads, what he watches on telly, the noise he makes when he sucks his teeth, I can smell his shaving lather, the sweat on him when he comes in from work; he's there, just like you're there but he's not. You want his name?

JULIA: His –

TRACY: Name? He's –

She tries to shape a name, closes her mouth again –

Be with you in a minute – don't go away –

Irritated with herself, she swats at the side of her head –

Eeejit eejit eejit eejit eejit –

TRACY shows signs of losing it, rocking from side to side –

Stupid head stupid head stupid head stupid head stupid
head stupid head stupid head –

TRACY pulls her notebook out, starts looking through it, puzzled –

Name name name name name name name name name
name name name name name name name name –

She throws the notebook onto the floor.

(*To JULIA.*) My head got broke in two. It's all got mixed
up, inside –

She picks up the notebook again –

Name name name name name name name name name
name name –

She throws it down.

I'm looking for his name but I know he's not there but
he is but he isn't because I've got two halves of a head
instead of a whole one –

She picks the notebook up again, leafs through it –

Name name name name name name name name name
name name –

She throws it onto the floor again.

(*To JULIA.*) And one half says one thing and one says
another and they can't both be right but they can be and
they are, even though they're not. Which doesn't mean
that I'm out of my head, or the two halves of my head –

She picks the notebook up again, leafs through it –

Name name name name name name name name name name name –

She throws it onto the floor again, exhausted.

(*To JULIA.*) In time this'll sort itself out, *they say, so they tell me,* or maybe it won't but right now I have to live with him though I don't because that's just how it is since I stopped a brick and if I know he's there even though I know he's not, how do I know you're not not-there, even though you are. You see what I mean? How do I know I'm not just talking to the wall when I'm talking to you? Could you be here and not here at the same time? Like he is. How would I know? You see why I'm so scared? I know that things shouldn't *be there* and *not be there* at the same time. I know that. Every sinner knows that. That's not how it's meant to be. Or is it? But it's what I'm stuck with. Or am I?

She turns to JIMMY –

Who is he? Or who isn't he?

TRACY nods, takes a deep breath, sits, hugging her knees, looking scared and vulnerable.

That's what I'd like to know. Although it's me making him up. Well I am but it's not me, it's my sick head. Here's here now. Although he's not –

JIMMY: (*Sings.*) *I wish I was in Carrickfergus*
Only for nights in Ballygrant –

TRACY picks up the song –

TRACY: *I would swim over the deepest ocean*

For my love to find –

JIMMY / TRACY: *But the sea is wide and I cannot cross over*
And neither have I the wings to fly –
I wish I could meet a handsome boatsman
To ferry me over to my love and die.

My childhood days bring back sad reflections
Of happy times I spent so long ago –

TRACY: Sure it's a terrible sad song, isn't it? And they're all like that –

JIMMY: *My boyhood friends and my own relations*
Have all passed on now like melting snow –

TRACY: I mean, even when they're happy, they're miserable, aren't they? The Irish. But I love him.

She suddenly swats the side of her head –

Eeejit eejit eejit eejit eejit eejit eejit eejit eejit –

But he's not there at all, I'm just talking to thin air, talking through me hat, talking out of me arse, making an arse of meself with me sick head –

She starts swatting her head with both hands –

My sick sick sick sick sick sick sick sick head – but he is there and I'm not just talking to the wall but I am and he isn't because I got hit by a brick and there's *no* wee flat, and he *doesn't* sleep with me but he *does* and he *is* and he wants the best for me, but he doesn't give a damn because I made him up –

She brandishes the pill box and bottle of Jameson –

You saw us? Me?

JULIA: Yes.

TRACY: What I was doing? Him and me?

JULIA: Yes.

TRACY: You stood and watched?

JULIA: The door was –

TRACY: You *knew* what I was doing? Us?

JULIA: Yes.

TRACY: Did nothing about it?

JULIA: No.

TRACY: Sat on your hunkers?

JULIA: My –?

TRACY: You'll *do* nothing about it?

JULIA: Why would I…?

TRACY: Why?

JULIA: Why?

TRACY: Why? The pills and –?

She mimes swallowing pills and chugging whiskey.

JULIA: I was in my car one day…and I'm still stuck…

TRACY: If you saw me doing it again would you try to stop me?

JULIA: I don't –

TRACY: It's against the rules here, you know. To – with the pills. Or anything else.

JULIA: Oh –

TRACY: You'd stand and watch? Again?

JULIA: When you get…stuck where…I got stuck…when you lose what I…lost when…that goes…

TRACY: (*Impatient again.*) Hm hm hm hm hm hm hm hm hm hm hm.

I'm having his baby.

JULIA: That's –

TRACY: No reason not, is there? I've an imaginary boyfriend – I might as well have an imaginary kiddie, too. Twins. More. As many as I like. Sixteen. Twenty. Lots of imaginary wee skitters running around in their imaginary wee shoes after their imaginary dad, whose having all this imaginary sex with me. Which would be better than the real thing any day, wouldn't it? I mean, if I want kids, they're going to have to be imaginary ones, aren't they? Now? Since I stopped a brick? I mean, take a gander.

She spreads her arms wide, feet planted apart under the shapeless dress –

I might have got a hole in my head but I know. I *know*. You know what I mean? When I say *I know?* I'm not having any kids. Unless it's with him over there in my head.

She wildly swings an imaginary baby in her arms –

Toora loora laddy
Toora loorah li
Toora loorah laddy
Is an Irish lullaby –

As if the baby has shot out of her arms –

Whoops – where'd the little bugger go?

She breaks off, looks closely at JULIA –

What's it like, do you think? Inside? Up here? If you were real? A real person?

JULIA: A real –?

TRACY: What did you say your name was?

JULIA: Julia.

TRACY: You know who you are, do you, Julia Peculia?

JULIA: I know…Julia…I know –

TRACY: And who you are inside? Or what's left of inside?

JULIA: I know…me…I know…

TRACY: I don't know who I am, I don't know if there's anybody there to *be* an AM but I know this isn't me, it wasn't who I was, it wasn't who I want to be, who I was going to be and I don't know who that is – (*JIMMY.*) – and what he's doing in my life or where he comes from or what he wants from me and sometimes I ask myself am I making him up or is he making me up because I'm not sure there's anybody here, most of the time. *You.* Do you know you're there? Or did you lose yourself somewhere? And you're still looking? When you're lying in bed with the pillow on your face aren't you trying to remember where you put yourself? Aren't you scared stiff that when you look in the mirror one day –

She pulls the mirror quickly out –

There'll be nobody looking back at you?

JULIA: I got stuck –

TRACY: Yeah?

JULIA: I'm still stuck –

TRACY: Yeah?

JULIA: And I'm not sure –

TRACY: Yeah?

JULIA: If I'll make it –

TRACY: Yeah?

JULIA: But it's different –

TRACY: Yeah?

JULIA: There are things called…words…which are the… names of…other…things…called feelings…I can't feel… these things…I will never…feel them…I will not feel… happy or…sad…or angry or upset…or…ever again…I can't feel what…these words for these things mean…I will not even feel…that I am…missing something because…to miss something you need…to remember what…having it must have been…like…or be able to tell…from what other people…tell you…what it is like to…have these things…which I can…never have now…

JULIA forces herself on –

> Nothing is better than…anywhere is the same as…is…
> *here…not here*…it doesn't matter to me…for you…it…
> matters…for you…I think…you know what these…
> words mean…I think you know…*to be happy…to be
> sad…joy…love…*

She forces herself to concentrate –

> I can't be your…friend…I don't have that…it's not…it
> can't be about…that…I don't…I know I should care…I
> know one of the reasons I'm…why they thought this
> would…for me…but before you…to want something you
> have to…to know what *to want* means…this is one of
> these…words I don't…I don't need a friend…that means
> to know *I need*…and I…don't have that…like you don't
> connect… chair and…the word for chair…I don't know
> *to care*…I don't know *to…miss*…I don't know…*to love*…
> and I don't care…what happened to you, who…the
> brick…fair I don't care…why they did that I don't…care
> about what happened to me not…really…so why should
> I…you and…the brick…it's all…stuck…and I don't
> know if I want to…unstick it because why…bother why
> when…you wanted me to see…that see the…pills…
> the…drink the…why you…why you left the door…open
> for me to see…that…

TRACY: I did not.

JULIA: Yes.

TRACY: No.

JULIA: Yes.

TRACY: I didn't –

JULIA: The door…

TRACY: No –

JULIA: Open…

TRACY: No –

JULIA: For me to…

TRACY: No –

JULIA: To stop…

TRACY: No –

JULIA: Stop…

TRACY: No –

JULIA: Stop you…

TRACY's pulled away from her, aggressive again –

TRACY: I don't need a friend. Did I ask you? Did I say? I've been here six months without one. So why now? Do I look that desperate?

She mocks how JULIA speaks –

Friend…I…know…you…make you my…I got hit by a… (*Indicates JIMMY.*) I've got him – I've got what I need –

To JIMMY –

Would you credit it? (*Mocking JULIA again.*) *I think you know…to be happy…to be…*

Isn't that so sad but up your hole with a big jam roll, I don't need you or anybody –

She grabs JIMMY's arm, possessive, proud of him –

I've come this far, by myself, with him. I try I try, I try so hard, every day I try and I try and I try and I try because I'm sick of it, so sick of it, sick sick sick sick sick sick sick of it –

She looks near despair again –

And I get so far and I think I'm getting somewhere and then I fuck up time after time, I know I do, I get so far and I fuck it up real bad, real real bad but at least I try, okay, I *try*, I don't just stand there – (*Mocking JULIA again.*) *To miss something you need...to remember what...*

It's like trying to shinny up an iceberg, I'm looking for something to hold on to and if I make it today, I've got it all to do again the next –

JIMMY: *Nothing is better than...anywhere is the same as...*

TRACY: But if I'm who I am because of where I come from – (*JIMMY.*) And he's him because of where he –

JIMMY: If we're *the bloody Irish* –

TRACY: Yeah –

JIMMY: If it's *oh the Irish* –

TRACY: *The Irish again*– then couldn't it be *the bloody English*, too –?

JIMMY: There's your Irish joke and your Scots joke and your Welsh joke but the English joke? There's Jock and there's Paddy and there's Taff – but the English are just the English, aren't they?

TRACY: Face it, love. You're just not funny.

JIMMY: You go into a bar and there they are with their big long faces. Like big white turds on legs. Like big white turds on legs with all the life boiled out of them.

If we're *the bloody Irish* –

TRACY: Yeah –

JIMMY: If it's *oh the Irish* –

TRACY: *The Irish* –

JIMMY: *The Irish again* –

TRACY: Somebody slung a brick and he's still walking around out there and I'm here, he didn't do a day inside and I got life because I'm walking down the street, minding my own business –

JIMMY: Only the end of it's blocked off because there's a march taking place –

TRACY mimes a swaggering march, sings –

TRACY: *It was old but it was beautiful*
The colors they were fine –

JIMMY: Only this time the people who live in the street have had enough and they're going to do something about it –

TRACY: And the polis have been called out, so they tell me, and it's bugger all to do with me –

JIMMY: But this lot runs this way and this lot runs that way and the bobbies run here and the others run there and I'm caught in the middle –

TRACY: When the tear gas comes flying in and they're banging their shields and this lot are yelling and shoving and that lot are yelling and shoving and the stones are starting to fly –

JIMMY: And just for a minute there I don't know which way to run, that must have been it, I must have been trying to figure where I'd be safe, which lot were which, what side I had to run to –

TRACY: Although I tried never to take sides, I just tried to get on with my own life, get on with my knitting but there I am, they think –

JIMMY: That's how it must have happened, the polis are coming one way and I'm caught in the middle and do I go with these lot or these lot, where'd I be safe, what side of the street should I be on, where do I stand? –

TRACY: When for thirty years I've been trying not to take one but *here it is* must have been going through my head, which of these bunches of eejits who're trying to kill each other is mine, what side of the line am I on, *now*, when I don't have a choice not to make one and then somebody slings a brick –

She makes one of her huge efforts to control herself –

I'm trying. Every day I'm trying, I'm trying, I'm trying, it's so hard but I'm trying, every minute of the day, and I need to be around people who are trying too, I don't need them to *be my friend,* that's not what I'm asking, I don't think I'm asking that, it's just that I can't do this by myself, with him, by myself, with him –

With a huge effort she stops herself –

I don't know the stakes that you're playing for, love, but I know mine. And I can't let anything get in my way because if I lose this where'll I be? Lying up there with a pillow over my head again?

Despairing –

But I might as well be, mightn't I? Because somebody did this to me and I won't let it go let it go let it go let it go let it go I won't I won't because you can't just stop a brick and it not mean something, stop a brick with your head your head your head your sick head, your sick sick head –

She straightens up, starts to pace agitatedly, humming under her breath, skipping, as if about to lose it again –

I'm looking for the sense in it, do you see? Why I ended up a headcase?

She slaps the side of her head –

Headcase headcase headcase headcase headcase headcase headcase headcase headcase –

She pulls out the mirror –

I don't know who that is but it's not me. This is me –

She grabs a makeup case, takes our the lipstick and smears it on her mouth. She slaps blush on her cheeks, mascara under her eyes.

Me me me me me me me me me me me me me me me me me me me me me me me me me me me me me me me me me –

She turns her face to him, grotesque with make-up. She starts to pace again, rubbing her hands together frantically, kicking off the boots and anorak, dumping the handbag on the floor.

JIMMY: You're making an arse of yourself again, aren't you, a right arse, an even bigger arse than usual, you're screwing up again real bad, real bad, real bad, real real real real real real real real real real read real real real real real real real real bad –

She rubs some of the makeup off.

Silly cow, silly silly silly silly silly silly silly silly silly silly silly silly cow –

She grabs a tissue and rubs the make-up off, smearing it even more grotesquely over her face.

Stupid bitch, stupid stupid stupid stupid stupid stupid stupid stupid stupid stupid bitch –

She's rubbing her face frantically as he goads her –

Where's the use where's the use where's the use where's the use –

She claps her hands over her ears, chants, trying to drown out anything he might say –

TRACY: Na na na na na na na na na na na na na na na –

She takes her hands off her ears –

I got hit by a brick –

Her hands over her ears again –

Na na na na na na na –

Off her ears –

Did you know that?

On her ears –

Na na na na na na na na na –

Off her ears –

B-R-I-C-K. Brick.

On her ears –

Na na na na na na na na na na –

Off her ears –

A brick is the word for a thing that is a brick. The thing called a brick hit my head.

On her ears –

Na na na na na na na na na na na na na na na –

Off her ears again –

There is no other word for a brick than brick.

On her ears –

Na na na na na na na –

Off her ears, talking faster and faster –

There are things called words which are the names of things called bricks. Did you know that? B R I C K. There is no such thing as a word, not really, not like there's a thing called a brick. We just call it a brick. This is what we call a brick. A brick. B R I C K. So we know what to call it. But the word for brick isn't real, the way the brick is. You can throw a brick. You can't throw the word for brick. It isn't there. Not in the same way. It's all very simple really. Do you understand it? Do you understand any of it? I don't. S H O E S. Shoes. Shoes is the word for shoes. If there wasn't the word for them they'd still be there. Or would they? But they wouldn't be shoes. Chair is the word for chair. C H A I R. You sit on a chair. But you don't. Because there's no such thing. As a chair. Well there is. Something you sit on. But there's no word for it unless you make one up. Chair is the word they've made up for chair. T R A C Y. That spells Tracy. Tracy is a word for somebody called Tracy. They've made that word up, too. There is no such thing as that word. Unless you say there is. When you say Tracy you have made up a word. That word is called a name. N A M E. Some words are called that. They are the names of people or things. A name is something that tells you what that thing is. That that thing is there. There are no names for things that aren't there. If a thing has a name it's there. T R A C Y. Tracy. Because that is Tracy's name she is there. She must be. That is the proof that Tracy exists. A name is given to something that is there. Tracy is not a shoe. S H O E. A shoe doesn't know whether it is there or not. On the other hand. It just is. Whether it's called a shoe or not. Because it isn't a shoe. Not really. It is not a word, it is a thing. A thing called a shoe. Tracy should know whether she is there or not. Because she is not a shoe or a chair. C H A I R. She is different to them. Tracy should know she's here. She *must* know. I am Tracy. T R A C Y. That is my name. That is the thing which does not exist which tells me that I do. Because I am here. With my name. This is very hard to understand. I have a hard time understanding this because somebody slung a brick at me –

JULIA: And so…so what?

TRACY: So what?

JULIA: So…so what?

TRACY: Somebody *did* this. It didn't just *happen.*

JULIA: There's…nothing you can do…about what happened to you…like I can't…do it either…you got hit by a…I…forgot my seat belt…once…just once…but you have to…I have to let…it go because…

I'm not stupid there's…nothing missing in my…it's the bit of me that…*feels* that's…when I hit the windscreen when I…broke my head in two like you…did…what I lost was…*feeling*…was…not my brain not my…mind lost my…that's what went…my soul I…think I lost…my soul and I think you lost…yours too…and we're…we have to find our…soul again –

TRACY: The only soul I know, missis, is me arsehole –

JULIA: I don't think we should have…a competition in…pointlessness but if we did I'd…win hands down what…happened to…you…like what happened to…me had no…meaning…there was no…point to it…there was…no reason for…either of those things to…happen…and when they happened there was no…point in them happening…so there's no point in you or me trying to…find one…

TRACY: Had your say, have you? Got that off your chest?

JULIA: Getting better isn't the point…the point of…finding your…finding your soul…

TRACY: Is that right?

JULIA: Even if…we're always going to…be worse off in every way…

TRACY: Says you.

JULIA: Than if we…hadn't had it happen…to…

TRACY: Says you –

JULIA: We were headed…over *there* and we ended up
  here…and we can't fool…ourselves it's…any different…

TRACY: You say –

JULIA: Not having bad…things happen to you is better
  than…having them happen to you –

TRACY: You say –

JULIA: Rising…above it all isn't…a patch on not
  having…to…but I can't do…and you can't…stay the girl
  who got…hit by the…brick the rest of your life…

JIMMY: You stuck up bitch –

TRACY: English –

JIMMY: Bitch –

TRACY: You stuck up English –

JIMMY: Bitch –

*JIMMY and TRACY start to grab JULIA's possessions, stuff them
back in the case –*

TRACY: You come in here, you bitch, you –

JIMMY: Keep your nose –

TRACY: Out of –

JIMMY: If you know what's good for you –

TRACY: Or you might get it fixed with a hammer –

JIMMY: And that's telling you –

TRACY: *So what?* SO WHAT?

JIMMY: No point to it?

TRACY and JIMMY begin to make the same physical actions as they harangue JULIA and pile her possessions up – we're seeing the perfect fusing of TRACY with her imaginary entity, performing each motion and gesture in a weird synchronization –

TRACY: And me with my sick head –

JIMMY/TRACY: My sick sick head – sick sick sick sick head –

JIMMY: My poor sick head –

JIMMY/TRACY: Sick sick sick sick – sick sick sick sick – sick sick sick sick –

JIMMY: Sick sick sick sick –

TRACY: Sick sick sick sick –

JIMMY / TRACY: Head, my head, my sick head – my poor sick head –

JIMMY: *So what –?*

TRACY: You bitch –

JIMMY: You stuck up –

TRACY: English –

JIMMY: Bitch, you bitch you –

TRACY and JIMMY are getting more and more excited, bouncing up and down, in tandem, their movements still in sync –

TRACY: Who says I want to be a Normie, anyway?
    Maybe I don't want to –

They mock a normal walk, holding themselves stiffly upright –

   How do you do?

They stick their hands out with a forced smile on their faces –

JIMMY: *Tickled, I'm sure –*

They giggle, let their bodies sway from side to side, making those excited noises in the backs of their throats –

TRACY: Maybe I'd rather be an eejit? Maybe I'd rather –

They walk around the room, legs shooting out in all directions, madly swinging their arms –

   What's so bad about that?

They stop, grinning, out of breath –

JIMMY: What's so bad about –

They throw themselves onto the chairs, rocking violently, grabbing their ankles, making noises in the backs of their throats –

TRACY: Maybe I'd rather be –

They jump to their feet, walking around the room, arms swinging, legs wide –

   Yakking and yakking and yakking and yakking –

JIMMY: And yakking and yakking and yakking and
    yakking –

TRACY: And yakking and yakking –

JIMMY/TRACY: And yakking and yakking –

They bounce around the room –

The thing is, you see, one of the things is, if I keep yakking, if I keep saying things, like, anything at all, the first thing that comes into my head, something like *See, if I keep yakking, if I keep saying things, anything at all, the first thing that comes into my head* – if I keep doing that – and maybe I'm doing it right now, right this minute, this very minute, maybe saying the first thing that comes into my head right now, here and now –

They give a little skip –

T-R-A-C-Y –

That's me. T-R-A-C-Y spells Tracy. Tracy is the name of a person. C-H-A-I-R spells chair. You sit on a chair. A chair is something you sit on.

They move to the chair, demonstrating –

Sit –

They sit, then spring to their feet again –

Sit –

They sit, then spring to their feet again –

Sit –

They, squirming and rocking from side to side, while rubbing their hands on their legs.

Something happened to me. I know that. If you ask me what it was –

They swat the sides of their heads –

Eejit eejit eejit eejit eejit eejit eejit eejit eejit eejit eejit eejit eejit eejit –

They stop abruptly, peer at their feet –

S-H-O-E-S. That spells shoes. You wear shoes. Shoes is the word for shoes. There is no other word for shoes. I am wearing shoes. The thing called a word for the things called shoes is shoes. Those are your shoes –

They rock even more violently, he rubs his hands on his legs, rocking backwards and forwards as well as from side to side –

When you get a brain injury it wouldn't be like having a broken leg, would it? You've got a broken leg –

You get out of bed, you fall on the floor –

They topple to the floor from the chair –

Jesus – what was that? Oh I remember now, I broke my leg –

TRACY jumps up –

TRACY: Go –

JIMMY gets to his feet –

JIMMY: Go –

TRACY: Just go –

JIMMY: Go –

They thrust JULIA's possessions at her –

TRACY: Here –

JIMMY: Not here –

TRACY: It's all the same, isn't it? –

JIMMY: For you –

TRACY: So go –

JIMMY: Go –

TRACY: Go –

JIMMY: Go –

TRACY: Go –

JIMMY: Go –

TRACY: Go –

JULIA exits, clutching her case. A plastic bag flies in, hovers. JIMMY stares at it.

JIMMY: Could you beat a one of those, in the heel of the hunt? If you'd made your mind up –

He takes it as she sits, as if all her strength and resistance has gone –

    Practical, ubiquitous – a choice of colors, a range of styles – above all sturdy, efficient and airtight –

He takes out something else –

What have we here?

It's a roll of tape –

A very handy thing around the house, a roll of sticky tape – you'd never know when you'd be needing it.

He holds out the bag –

Shall we try them on for size? Now you're sure –?

She nods, as if too tired to argue. He hands her the bag. She places it on her head as he sings –

Where Lagan streams sing lullaby
There blows a lily fair
The twilight gleam is in her eye
The night is on her hair –

She holds up her finger. He wraps tape around it.

And like a love-sick lenashee
She hath my soul in thrall
No life have I, nor liberty
For love is Lord of all –

He starts to circle her, unspooling the tape –

And often when the beetle's horn
Has lulled the eye to sleep
I slip into her shieling lorn
And through the doorway creep –

The tape fastens around the bag, starting to choke her –

There on the cricket's singing stone
She makes the bogwood fire
Then comes that soft sweet undertone

The song of heart's desire –

TRACY's body heaves as she struggles for breath. Then she reaches for the bag, tears it off her head, gasping.

TRACY: Go you.

JIMMY: What?

TRACY: Go.

JIMMY: I won't.

TRACY: *Go.*

JIMMY: No I won't.

TRACY: You have to go now because…because I want you to go.

JIMMY: Fuck that. There's this guy goes into a bar –

TRACY: *No.*

JIMMY: This pal of mine –

TRACY: *No.*

JIMMY: There's these two nuns –

TRACY: *No.*

JIMMY: *From Bantry Bay to –*

He sings, pushes the pill towards her –

> *From Bantry Bay to the Derry Quay –*

TRACY: No.

JIMMY: Yes.

TRACY: I'm telling you…you have to go…

She takes out the mirror, holds it towards him –

That's not me –

She lets her arm with the mirror hang at her side –

This is me –

She holds the mirror out to him again –

That's not –

She lets it hang at her side again –

This is –

She holds it out again –

She's –

She lets it hang at her side again –

I'm – and you go now –

JIMMY: No.

TRACY: Yes.

She drops the mirror on the floor, puts her foot on it, breaks it.

So go.

JIMMY: Fuck it.

TRACY heads to the couch. She lifts off the seat cushions.

TRACY: Get in –

JIMMY: No.

TRACY: Get in.

JIMMY: I won't.

TRACY: You will.

JIMMY: I won't.

TRACY: You will.

JIMMY: No I won't.

TRACY: Yes, you will.

JIMMY heads reluctantly to the couch, steps into it.

JIMMY: Fuck this.

TRACY: Do it.

JIMMY: No.

TRACY: You will you will you will.

Standing in the couch he sings, appealing –

JIMMY: *I love you like I never loved before*
   When first I met you on the village green –

TRACY: Get down –

He lies flat, keeps singing, even though he's out of sight inside the couch –

JIMMY: *Come to me ere my dream of love is o'er –*

TRACY puts the first cushion back. He keeps singing –

   I love you like I loved you –

She puts the second cushion back. The couch is an ordinary item of furniture again – except for the muffled voice coming from it –

When you were sweet – when you were sweet – sixteen –

Silence. The door opens and JULIA is standing there, case in hand. TRACY doesn't look at her.

TRACY: Tracy was going to do it, this time. This time it was for real. No more footering around. This was it. All the other times she was just an oul cod. But this was –

She looks at the Scotch and the bottle of pills –

The whole shooting match. In the room by herself. She wasn't just up her own arse picking blackberries, not this time, no.

But this time, it wasn't Tracy. It was me.

She looks down at the broken mirror –

Me –

She kneels, starts to pick up the pieces of the mirror and set them down again –

Tracy…Tracy Tracy Tracy…

She looks at the pattern of fragments on the floor –

You poor bloody eejit, you –

She touches them, moves them into another pattern –

You daft bugger –

She looks up at JULIA, her diction like JULIA's painful, halting speech –

I got…hit by a…brick and…it all went…up here…inside like…snow off a ditch…and…I didn't know who I was for a…while or if…there was anybody there at all and…I'm still not all the way…back…not yet and I don't know…if I ever will all…not all the way…but…

She gets to her feet, leaving the shards of mirror on the floor –

I'm not a…shoe I'm not…a chair…and I'm not…not Tracy…

She shakes her head, trying to clear it –

I'm not yon poor wee eejit not…

She mimes writing the name tags and sticking them onto her –

T R A C Y … T R A C Y … T R A C Y …

She stops the mime –

I'm real I'm…a person I'm…I'm me –

She indicates the case in JULIA's hand –

You want a hand with that?

JULIA: I don't…I've nowhere to…I'm trying too…

TRACY: I guess we're stuck with each other, aren't we?

JULIA: I don't…I…

TRACY: Ah shut your mouth and give your arse a chance –

She takes the case and heads away –

Are you coming in or are you going to stand there all day with your hair in curlers and fish and chips in your hand?

She opens the case, starts to take JULIA's possessions out –

(*Warning.*) I'm going to miss your man, don't think I'm not.

Sings –

*I wish I was in Carrickfergus
Only for nights in Ballygrant –*

She stops, looks around the room, as if to make sure JIMMY has gone for good –

Sure he was good crack – but you can't have imaginary wee skitters running around inside your head, can you? Even if they've got a gag for every day of the week.

She hesitates, looks at the things she's taken from the suitcase –

You should be doing this –

She puts them back, hands the case to JULIA. As JULIA unpacks TRACY hums Carrickfergus, *watching –*

What'd you say your name was?

JULIA: Julia –

TRACY sticks her hand out –

TRACY: I'm me.

The lights start to dim on JULIA, isolating TRACY –

I'm Irish…

Beat –

But I'm getting over it....

She hums Carrickfergus *as the lights fade and we –*

end